Revocation of a Living Trust Kit

EstateBee

By EstateBee Publishing

Bibliographic Data

- International Standard Book Number (ISBN): 978-1-913889-09-8
- Printed in the United States of America
- First Edition: December 2010
- Second Edition: January 2014
- Third Edition: September 2020

Published By: EstateBee Limited,
23 Lynn Road,
London SW12 9LB,
United Kingdom

Printed and Distributed By: Kindle Direct Publishing, an Amazon Company

For more information, e-mail books@estate-bee.com.

Important Note

This kit is meant as a general guide to revoking a living trust. While effort has been made to make this kit as accurate as possible, laws and their interpretation are constantly changing. As such, you are advised to update this information with your own research and/or counsel and to consult with your personal legal, financial, and/or medical advisors before acting on any information contained in this kit.

The purpose of this kit is to educate and entertain. It is not meant to provide legal, financial, or medical advice or to create any attorney-client or other advisory relationship. The authors and publisher shall have neither liability (whether in negligence or otherwise) nor responsibility to any person or entity with respect to any loss or damage caused or alleged to be caused directly or indirectly by the information contained in this kit or the use of that information.

About EstateBee

EstateBee, the international self-help legal publisher, was founded in 2000 by lawyers from one of the most prestigious international law firms in the World.

Our aim was simple - to provide access to quality legal information and products at an affordable price.

Our will writing software was first published in that year and, following its adaptation to cater for the legal systems of various countries worldwide, quickly drew more than 40,000 visitors per month to our website. From this humble start, EstateBee has quickly grown to become a leading international estate planning and asset protection self-help publisher with legal titles in the United States, Canada, the United Kingdom, Australia, and Ireland.

Our publications provide customers with the confidence and knowledge to help them deal with everyday estate planning issues such as the preparation of a last will and testament, a living trust, a power of attorney, administering an estate and much more.

By providing customers with much needed information and forms, we enable them to place themselves in a position where they can protect both themselves and their families using easy to read legal documents and forward planning techniques.

The Future….

We are always seeking to expand and improve the products and services we offer. However, to do this, we need to hear from interested authors and to receive feedback from our customers.

If something isn't clear to you in one of our publications, please let us know and we'll try to make it clearer in the next edition. If you can't find the answer you want and have a suggestion for an addition to our range, we'll happily look at that too.

Using Self-Help Kits

Before using a self-help kit, you need to carefully consider the advantages and disadvantages of doing so – particularly where the subject matter is of a legal or tax related nature.

In writing our self-help kits, we try to provide readers with an overview of the laws in a specific area, as well as some sample documents. While this overview is often general in nature, it provides a good starting point for those wishing to carry out a more detailed review of a topic.

However, unlike an attorney advising a client, we cannot cover every conceivable eventuality that might affect our readers. Within the intended scope of this kit, we can only cover the principal areas in each topic, and even where we cover these areas, we can still only do so to a moderate extent. To do otherwise would result in the writing of a textbook which would be capable of use by legal professionals. This is not what we do.

We try to present useful information and documents that can be used by an average reader with little or no legal knowledge. While our sample documents can be used in most cases, everybody's personal circumstances are different. As such, they may not be suitable for everyone. You may have personal circumstances which might impact the effectiveness of these documents or even your desire to use them. The reality is that without engaging an attorney to review your personal circumstances, this risk will always exist. It's for this very reason that you need to consider whether the cost of using a do-it-yourself legal document outweighs the risk that there may be something special about your particular circumstances which might not be taken into account by the sample documents attached to this kit (or indeed any other sample documents).

It goes without saying (we hope) that if you are in any doubt as to whether the documents in this kit are suitable for use in your particular circumstances, you should contact a suitably qualified attorney for advice before using them. Remember the decision to use these documents is yours. We are not advising you in any respect.

In using this kit, you should also consider the fact that this kit has been written with the purpose of providing a general overview of the laws in the United States. As such, it does not attempt to cover all the various procedural nuances and specific requirements that may apply from state to state – although we do point some of these out along the way. Rather, in our kit, we try to provide forms which give a fair example of the type of forms which are commonly used in most states. Nevertheless, it remains possible that your state may have specific requirements which have not been taken into account in our forms.

Another thing that you should remember is that the law changes – thousands of new laws are brought into force every day and, by the same token, thousands are repealed or amended every day. As such, it is possible that while you are reading this kit, the law might well have been changed. We hope it hasn't, but the chance does exist. To address this, when we become aware of them, we do send updates to our customers about material changes to the law. We also ensure that our books are reviewed and revised regularly to take account of these changes.

Anyway, assuming that all the above is acceptable to you, let's move on to exploring the topic at hand.........revoking a living trust.

Table of Contents

Revocation of a Living Trust

What Are Living Trusts?

A revocable living trust is a type of 'inter vivos' trust (a trust made between living people) used for estate planning purposes. Under a revocable living trust agreement, you as the creator of the living trust, declare yourself trustee of the trust and then transfer some or all your personal property to the trust. The legal ownership of the property passes from you personally to the trust. However, as trustee of the trust you maintain control over and use of the trust property.

As creator of the revocable living trust, you can, at any time, either revoke the living trust or call for the return of some or all the property transferred to it. You can also add assets to the trust, change the terms of the trust and even make it irrevocable (incapable of change) at any time in the future.

After your death, the assets in the revocable living trust will pass to the beneficiaries that you have named in the living trust agreement in much the same way that they would under a last will and testament. Specifically, your living trust agreement will nominate a person known as the "successor trustee" (which is a little like an executor or personal representative) who will have the responsibility of transferring ownership of the assets in the trust to the beneficiaries named in the trust document following your death. In most cases, the whole transfer process takes only a few weeks.

Revocation of a Living Trust

Revocation is the legal name given to the termination or cancellation of an agreement, such as a living trust agreement. So long as you are not incapacitated, you can revoke or terminate your living trust at any time by sending a notice of revocation to the trustee(s) of the trust. This is a written notice signed by you as creator (grantor) of the living trust stating that you are terminating the living trust arrangement and calling for the trust assets be returned to the grantor(s). The notice of revocation should be addressed and sent to all trustees of the trust.

How to Revoke a Living Trust

To revoke a living trust, you will need to do the following: -

- Firstly, in your capacity as grantor, prepare and serve a notice of revocation on the trustee(s) of the living trust. As you will also be a trustee, you will (as the grantor) need to address the notice to yourself as trustee. The notice will inform the trustee(s) that the trust is being terminated and will call for the return of the trust assets to the grantor(s). A sample notice of revocation is contained at Appendix 2.

- Secondly, you must arrange to transfer the legal title in the trust assets back to the grantor(s) personally. We will discuss how you do this in the next section.

It is important to note that with a shared living trust or an AB trust, notwithstanding that there are normally two co-grantors, each co-grantor has the legal right to unilaterally terminate the living trust. The grantor can so this by serving a notice of revocation on the trustees of the trust. He or she does not need the signature of the second grantor to do this.

In tandem with transferring the trust assets back to the grantor(s), it is important to also ensure that any beneficiary designations made in favor of the living trust are amended. These designations could be designations under a pay-on-death account, transfer on death account, life insurance policy or indeed under any other account. If you do not amend the designations, there is a risk that the proceeds in the relevant account could be deemed to form part of your probate estate and could end up going to the residuary beneficiary named in your last will – which may not be something that was intended.

Sample forms have been included in the appendices to this kit to help you revoke a living trust. These forms include both a notice of revocation and a deed of assignment to legally transfer assets from the trust back to your own personal name. More information on transferring assets is set out in the next section.

Important Note

If you have any queries in relation to the specific process around revoking your living trust or in relation to the sample documents provided with this kit, you should speak to an attorney licensed in your state.

Transferring Trust Assets into Your Name

Assets in your living trust can be divided into two broad categories - those with formal title documents (such as real estate and vehicles) and those without (such as jewelry and antiques). The transfer of each these categories of assets will need to be documented in different ways for the transfers to have legal effect.

For assets without formal title documents, the transfer process is relatively straightforward. You simply need to sign a transfer document known as a deed of assignment or deed of transfer. The document will be entered into between the trustee(s) and grantor(s) of the trust and will set out details of the assets being transferred from the trust to the grantors. Once the transfer document is signed by all parties, it will have immediate legal effect and the transfer will have become legally effective. Sample deeds of assignment are contained at Appendix 3.

As you will see from the samples, the transfer documents are entered into between the grantor(s) and the trustee(s). For example, it could be between (1) John Smith, as trustee of the John Smith Family Living Trust dated 16 January 2009 and (2) John Smith. In this example, the signatory (John Smith) will be signing as both grantor and trustee of the living trust. While it may seem odd to have a person enter into an agreement with himself, it is perfectly normal in this instance as the signatory is signing in two separate legal capacities - grantor and trustee.

Turning to the transfer of assets that have formal title documents, these assets will need to be transferred in the manner that they are customarily transferred in your state - which is usually the reverse of how you transferred those assets into the living trust in the first instance. It is important to ensure that these transfers are done correctly as any failure to comply with the required formalities could result in the asset remaining in the living trust. A summary of the more common transfer mechanisms for assets with title documents is contained in the next section.

Once all the assets have been transferred out of the living trust, the living trust will (in most cases) automatically cease to exist.

Transferring Titled Assets from Your Trust

Given the vast diversity of assets that you could have transferred to your living trust, we take a very brief look below at some of the most commonly transferred assets and how you can go about re-registering the title to those assets in your own name. Remember - in most cases, all you will need to do is the reverse the process that you used to transfer those assets into the trust in the first place.

Real Estate

To transfer real estate from your living trust you will need to prepare a deed of transfer. In most cases this is relatively straightforward. However, there are certain issues that you need to watch out for as there are many different nuances associated with the transfer of title to real estate – such as the type of deed required, title insurance, mortgages, out-of-state property, homestead rights and tax on transfer deeds. As such, we recommend that you engage the services of an attorney qualified in your state to assist with the transfer of any property located in your state.

Important Note

Remember to notify your insurance company when re-registering real estate in your personal name. Any failure to do so could result in the property being un-insured.

Cars, Boats and Other Vehicles

You can transfer a vehicle from your trust in much the same way as you would transfer it to a third party. You should note that most states have a specific form that can be used for registering the transfer of a vehicle. You should locate the relevant form and complete it. Once completed, it will usually need to be registered with the Department of Motor Vehicles, or some other state department.

Cash Accounts

To re-transfer the title to any current (checking) accounts, savings accounts or money market accounts held by the trust, you can either change the name on the account (for example, from "John Smith, trustee of John Smith Family Living Trust" to "John Smith") or close the account and open a new one. The financial institution in which the account is held can advise you on which of the two methods they will allow. In each case, they will require evidence that the trust has been terminated. Normally, this can be satisfied by producing a copy of the signed notice of revocation.

United States Savings Bonds

While U.S. Savings bonds can be transferred to and from your living trust, you will need to contact your bank to obtain the appropriate form to transfer the bonds as well as details of the procedure involved. Once the transfer is completed, the bonds will be re-issued in your personal name.

Broker Accounts

It is also possible to transfer a broker account held with a brokerage firm or with a mutual fund company to and from your living trust. Similar to the position with bank accounts, you will need to contact the firm/company to determine whether they can simply change the name on the account or whether they will have to close the existing account and open a new one in your personal name.

Publicly Quoted Stocks and Bonds

There are two ways to transfer stock and bonds in a publicly quoted company from your living trust. You can contact the company's share registrar (or transfer agent as it's often called) or you can contact your broker and ask him to open an account in your personal name and have the stock and bonds re-issued in your name.

Retirement Plans

Due to their complexity, tax advantages and unique distribution features, pension plans, profit-sharing plans, IRSs, Keoghs, SEPs and other qualified pension plans should never be transferred into a living trust without first consulting your tax advisor. If you have transferred any such retirement plans to your living trust, you should speak to your tax advisor to determine the best way to transfer the plan back to your personal name.

Other Property

If you want to transfer any other property from your living trust, a simple deed of assignment should suffice. However, if there are specific transfer documents required to effect transfers of property (such as stock transfer forms for a corporation) then you should use the required form.

If you are uncertain as to how to proceed in relation to any specific asset transfer, we suggest that you speak to an attorney who will be able to guide you.

Appendices

Appendix 1

Signing Instructions

Completion Instructions for The Notice of Revocation of a Living Trust

1. On the cover page, insert the date of execution of the notice of revocation as well as your name as grantor in the spaces provided.
2. On page 1, enter your name and address, the date the trust was established and the date of execution of the notice of revocation. Sign your name as grantor in the space provided.
3. The final page of the agreement contains a notary affidavit. There is generally no requirement that you have a notary complete this affidavit. However, we recommend that you have it completed as it lessens the likelihood that your execution of the notice of revocation could be challenged by others. Simply bring the notice together with identification to a notary and he or she will be able to assist you with the remaining steps.

Completion Instructions for the Deed of Assignment for Use with a Revocable Living Trust for an Individual

1. On the cover page, insert the date of execution of the deed as well as your name as both trustee and grantor in the spaces provided. Remember, as you are most likely acting as both trustee and grantor, the deed will probably be between you (as trustee) and you (as grantor).
2. On page 1, enter the date of execution of the deed at the very top of the page.
3. The top half of page one identifies the parties to the deed. You should enter your name and address in the spaces provided for insertion in (1) and (2) (details of both the trustee and grantor respectively).
4. In Recital A, enter the date of creation of the trust and the name of the trust.
5. At clause 1.1, insert details of the assets you wish to transfer by deed of assignment from the trust to your personal name. Remember to be as specific as possible in describing the assets.

6. Print your name in the execution block on the last page and sign your name directly opposite the execution block in the space provided. You should sign your name in the presence of a witness. The witness should print and sign his/her name in the spaces provided under your execution block.

Completion Instructions for the Deed of Assignment for Use with a Revocable Living Trust for a Couple

1. On the cover page, insert the date of execution of the deed as well as your names as both trustees and grantors in the spaces provided. Remember, as you and your spouse are most likely trustees and grantors, the deed will be between you and your spouse (as trustees) and you and your spouse (as grantors).
2. On page 1, enter the date of execution of the deed at the very top of the page.
3. The top half of page one identifies the parties to the deed. You should enter your name and address and your spouse's name and address in the spaces provided for insertion in (1) and (2) (details of both the trustees and grantors respectively).
4. In Recital A, enter the date of creation of the trust and the name of the trust.
5. At clause 1.1, insert details of the assets you wish to transfer by deed of assignment from the trust to you or your spouse. Remember to be as specific as possible in describing the assets.

Important Note

If the asset held in the trust is to be transferred to only one of the spouses rather than both, then this needs to be specified in Clause 1.1. So, the transfer will be to the specific named spouse instead of to "the Grantors".

6. Print your name in the execution block on the last page and sign your name directly opposite the execution block in the space provided. You should sign your name in the presence of a witness. The witness should print and sign his/her name in the spaces provided under your execution block. You should repeat the process for our spouse.

Appendix 2

Notice of Revocation of a Living Trust

Downloadable Forms

Blank copies of this notice of revocation form can be downloaded from the EstateBee website. Simply login to your account or, if you don't have an account, you can create one for free.

www.estate-bee.com/login

Once logged in, go to your profile page and enter the code listed below in the 'Use Codes' tab:

REVLTKITNOT123

Notice of Revocation

of

____

(Grantor)

Dated this _____ day of __________________, 20____

Notice of Revocation

I, ______________________________ of ______________________________, as grantor under a Revocable Living Trust Agreement dated the ______ day of ______________, 20____ (the "Agreement") wherein you are designated as a trustee, or have been appointed successor trustee thereunder, do hereby revoke the powers and trusts created and conferred by me under the terms of the Agreement.

I hereby direct you, as trustee, to turn over and deliver to me all property held by you subject to the terms and provisions of the Agreement and to which I am entitled following this revocation, together with all accumulations of interest and income and any rights to which I am or ought to be beneficially entitled.

This REVOCATION is made this the ______ day of ______________, 20____.

____

Grantor

Notary Affidavit

State of ______________ County of ________________________

On ______________ before me, ________________________, a notary public, personally appeared ____________________________, who proved to me on the basis of satisfactory evidence to be the person whose name is subscribed to the within instrument and acknowledged to me that he/she executed the same in his/her authorized capacity, and that by his/her signature on the instrument the person executed the instrument. I certify under penalty of perjury that the foregoing is true and correct

Witness my hand and official seal.

Signature ______________________________

My Commission Expires:

____

(SEAL)

Appendix 3

Deeds of Assignment

(For Use With An Individual Revocable Living Trust)

Downloadable Forms

Blank copies of this deed of assignment form can be downloaded from the EstateBee website. Simply login to your account or, if you don't have an account, you can create one for free.

www.estate-bee.com/login

Once logged in, go to your profile page and enter the code listed below in the 'Use Codes' tab:

REVLTKITDAI123

Deed of Assignment

____
(Assignor/Grantor)

and

____
(Assignee/Grantee)

Dated this _____ day of _________________, 20____

Estate

www.estate-bee.com

Deed of Assignment

This Deed is made on this _____ day of ______________________, 20 ___.

Between:

(1) ______________________ of __________________________________ in his/her capacity as grantor of the Trust (the "**Grantor**"); and

(2) ______________________ of __________________________________ in his/her capacity as trustee of the Trust (the "**Trustee**").

Whereas:

A. Pursuant to a Revocable Living Trust Agreement dated day of 20___, made between the Grantor and the Trustee, the Grantor created a trust known as _________________ (the "**Trust**").

B. The Grantor is the legal and beneficial owner of the property described in Clause 1 below (the "**Property**").

C. The Grantor has agreed to assign all of the Grantor's rights, interests and entitlements in the Property to the Trust and the Trustee has agreed to accept such assignment subject to the terms and conditions of this Deed.

1. Assignment of Property

1.1 For good and valuable consideration (the receipt of which is hereby acknowledged), the Grantor hereby absolutely and unconditionally assigns all the Grantor's rights, entitlements, interests in and to the following property :-____

____

____

____

____

_________________________ the Trustee, as trustee of the Trust.

2. Binding on Successors

2.1 This Deed shall be binding upon and ensure to the benefit of the respective parties hereto and their respective personal representatives and successors.

3. Notice

3.1 Any notice or other communication given or made under this Deed shall be in writing and shall be delivered to the relevant party or sent by first class mail to the address of that party specified in this Deed or to such other address as may be notified hereunder by that party from time to time for this purpose.

3.2 Unless the contrary shall be proved, each such notice or communication shall be deemed to have been given, made and delivered, if by letter, 48 hours after posting or if by delivery, when left at the relevant address.

4. Counterparts

4.1 This Deed may be executed in any number of counterparts and by the different parties hereto on separate counterparts each of which when executed and delivered shall constitute an original and all such counterparts together constituting but one and the same instrument.

5. Severability

5.1 Each of the provisions of this Deed is separate and severable and enforceable accordingly and if at any time any provision is adjudged by any court of competent jurisdiction to be void or unenforceable the validity, legality and enforceability of the remaining provisions hereof and of that provision in any other jurisdiction shall not in any way be affected or impaired thereby.

6. Whole Agreement

6.1 This Deed contains the whole agreement between the parties hereto relating to the matters provided for in this Deed and supersedes all previous deeds or agreements (if any) between such parties in respect of such matters and each of the parties to this Deed acknowledges that in agreeing to enter into this Deed it has not relied on any representations or warranties except for those contained in this Deed.

As Witness the parties hereto have executed this document as a deed on the date appearing at the head hereof.

Executed and Delivered as a Deed

By ______________________________(print name)

As Grantor and Trustee ______________________________

(Signature)

In the presence of:

____

(Name of witness)

____

(Signature)

Deed of Assignment

(For Use With A Couple's Revocable Living Trust)

Downloadable Forms

Blank copies of this deed of assignment form can be downloaded from the EstateBee website. Simply login to your account or, if you don't have an account, you can create one for free.

www.estate-bee.com/login

Once logged in, go to your profile page and enter the code listed below in the 'Use Codes' tab:

REVLTKITDAC123

Deed of Assignment

__________________________and__________________________

(Assignors/Grantors)

and

__________________________and__________________________

(Assignees/Grantees)

Dated this _____ day of _________________, 20___

Deed of Assignment

This Deed is made on this ______ day of ____________________________, 20___.

Between:

(1) ______________________ of ________________________________ and ___________________________ of __________________________ in their capacity as grantors of the Trust (the "**Grantors**"); and

(2) ______________________ of ________________________________ and ___________________________ of __________________________ in their capacity as trustees of the Trust (the "**Trustees**").

Whereas:

A. Pursuant to a Revocable Living Trust Agreement dated day of 20___, made between the Grantors and the Trustees, the Grantors created a trust known as _______________ (the "**Trust**").

B. The Grantors (or either of them) are the legal and beneficial owners of the property described in Clause 1 below (the "**Property**").

C. The Grantors have agreed to assign all of their respective rights, interests and entitlements in the Property to the Trust and the Trustees have agreed to accept such assignment subject to the terms and conditions of this Deed.

1. Assignment of Property

1.1 For good and valuable consideration (the receipt of which is hereby acknowledged), the Grantors hereby absolutely and unconditionally assign all of their respective rights, entitlements, interests in and to the following property:

____

____

____

____

____

to the Trustees, as trustees of the Trust.

2. Binding on Successors

2.1 This Deed shall be binding upon and ensure to the benefit of the respective parties hereto and their respective personal representatives and successors.

3. Notice

3.1 Any notice or other communication given or made under this Deed shall be in writing and shall be delivered to the relevant party or sent by first class mail to the address of that party specified in this Deed or to such other address as may be notified hereunder by that party from time to time for this purpose.

3.2 Unless the contrary shall be proved, each such notice or communication shall be deemed to have been given, made and delivered, if by letter, 48 hours after posting or if by delivery, when left at the relevant address.

4. Counterparts

4.1 This Deed may be executed in any number of counterparts and by the different parties hereto on separate counterparts each of which when executed and delivered shall constitute an original and all such counterparts together constituting but one and the same instrument.

5. Severability

5.1 Each of the provisions of this Deed is separate and severable and enforceable accordingly and if at any time any provision is adjudged by any court of competent jurisdiction to be void or unenforceable the validity, legality and enforceability of the remaining provisions hereof and of that provision in any other jurisdiction shall not in any way be affected or impaired thereby.

6. Whole Agreement

6.1 This Deed contains the whole agreement between the parties hereto relating to the matters provided for in this Deed and supersedes all previous deeds or agreements (if any) between such parties in respect of such matters and each of the parties to this Deed acknowledges that in agreeing to enter into this Deed it has not relied on any representations or warranties except for those contained in this Deed.

As Witness the parties hereto have executed this document as a deed on the date appearing at the head hereof.

Executed and Delivered as a Deed

By ______________________________(print name)

As Grantor and Trustee ______________________________

(Signature)

In the presence of:

____

(Name of witness)

____

(Signature)

Executed and Delivered as a Deed

By ______________________________ (print name)

As Grantor and Trustee ______________________________

(Signature)

In the presence of:

____

(Name of witness)

____

(Signature)

EstateBee's Estate Planning Range

Make Your Own Last Will & Testament

Make Your Own Living Trust & Avoid Probate

Make Your Own Medical & Financial Power of Attorney

How to Probate an Estate - A Step-by-Step Guide for Executors

Estate Planning Essentials - A Step-by-Step Guide to Estate Planning

Funeral Planning Basics - A Step-by-Step Guide to Funeral Planning

Legal Will Kit

Living Trust Kit

Healthcare Power of Attorney & Living Will Kit

Codicil to a Last Will & Testament Kit

Durable General Power of Attorney Kit

Durable Limited Power of Attorney Kit

Made in United States
North Haven, CT
05 November 2026

21771706R00022